A SONG OF THE ENGLISH

WE ARE WAITING BY
THE TRAILS THAT
WE LOST

HEATH
ROBINSON.

A SONG OF THE ENGLISH
BY RUDYARD KIPLING
illustrated by
W. HEATH ROBINSON

CONTENTS

A SONG OF THE ENGLISH

VI. THE SONG OF THE CITIES :—

BOMBAY

Royal and Dower-royal, I the Queen.

CALCUTTA

Me the Sea-captain loved, the River built.

MADRAS

Clive kissed me on the mouth and eyes and brow.

RANGOON

Hail, Mother! Do they call me rich in trade?

SINGAPORE

Hail, Mother! East and West must seek my aid.

HONG-KONG

Hail, Mother! Hold me fast; my Praya sleeps.

A SONG OF THE ENGLISH

THE SONG OF THE CITIES—*Continued*

HALIFAX

Into the mist my guardian prows put forth.

QUEBEC AND MONTREAL

Peace is our portion. Yet a whisper rose.

VICTORIA

From East to West the circling word has passed.

CAPETOWN

Hail! Snatched and bartered oft from hand to hand.

MELBOURNE

Greeting! Nor fear nor favour won us place.

SYDNEY

Greeting! My birth-stain have I turned to good.

BRISBANE

The northern stirp beneath the southern skies.

THE SONG OF THE CITIES—*Continued.*

HOBART

Man's love first found me; man's hate made me Hell.

AUCKLAND

Last, loneliest, loveliest, exquisite, apart.

VII. ENGLAND'S ANSWER

Truly ye come of The Blood; slower to bless than to ban.

ILLUSTRATIONS IN COLOUR

7. Then the wood failed—then the food failed—then the last water dried—
   In the faith of little children we lay down and died.

8. On the sand-drift—on the veldt-side—in the fern-scrub we lay,
   That our sons might follow after by the bones on the way.

9. Follow after—follow after—for the harvest is sown:
   By the bones about the wayside ye shall come to your own!

10. When Drake went down to the Horn,
    And England was crowned thereby.

11. We have fed our sea for a thousand years,
    And she calls us, still unfed,
    Though there's never a wave of all her waves
    But marks our English dead.

12. If blood be the price of admiralty,
    Lord God, we ha' paid in full!

13. There's never a flood goes shoreward now
    But lifts a keel we manned;
    There's never an ebb goes seaward now
    But drops our dead on the sand—
    But slinks our dead on the sands forlore
    From the Ducies to the Swin.

14. The wrecks dissolve, above us; their dust drops down from afar—
Down to the dark, the utter dark, where the blind white sea-snakes are.

15. Here in the womb of the world—here on the tie-ribs of earth
Words, and the words of men, flicker and flutter and beat—
Warning, sorrow and gain, salutation and mirth—
For a Power troubles the Still that has neither voice nor feet.

16. Those that have stayed at thy knees, Mother, go call them in—
We that were bred overseas wait and would speak with our kin.
Not in the dark do we fight—haggle and flout and gibe;
Selling our love for a price, loaning our hearts for a bribe.

17. Bombay.

18. Calcutta.

19. Madras.

20. Rangoon.

21. Singapore.

22. Hong-Kong.

23. Halifax.

24. Quebec and Montreal.

25. Capetown.

26. Melbourne.

27. Sydney.

28. Hobart.

29. Auckland.

30. Deeper than speech our love, stronger than life our tether,
But we do not fall on the neck nor kiss when we come together.
My arm is nothing weak, my strength is not gone by;
Sons, I have borne many sons, but my dugs are not dry.

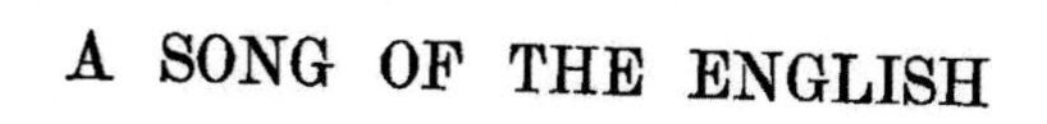

A SONG OF THE ENGLISH

II

HE HATH SMOTE FOR US A PATHWAY TO THE ENDS OF ALL THE EARTH

Fair is our lot—O goodly is our heritage!
(Humble ye, my people, and be fearful in your mirth!)
  For the Lord our God Most High
  He hath made the deep as dry,
He hath smote for us a pathway to the ends of all the Earth!

HE HATH SMOTE FOR US A
PATHWAY TO THE ENDS
OF ALL THE EARTH

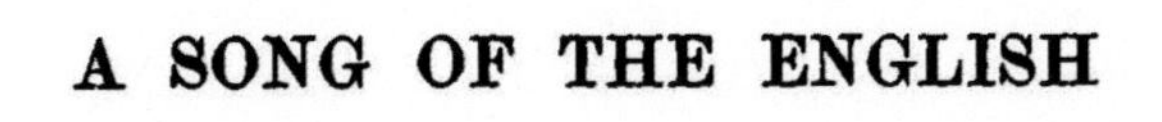
A SONG OF THE ENGLISH

Fair is our lot—O goodly is our heritage!
(Humble ye, my people, and be fearful in your
mirth!)
For the Lord our God Most High
He hath made the deep as dry,
He hath smote for us a pathway to the ends of all
the Earth!

Yea, though we sinned—and our rulers went from righteousness—
Deep in all dishonour though we stained our garments' hem.
Oh be ye not dismayed,
Though we stumbled and we strayed,
We were led by evil counsellors—the Lord shall deal with them!

Hold ye the Faith—the Faith our Fathers sealèd
us;
Whoring not with visions—overwise and over-
stale.
Except ye pay the Lord
Single heart and single sword,
Of your children in their bondage shall He ask
them treble-tale!

Keep ye the Law—be swift in all obedience—

Clear the land of evil, drive the road and bridge the ford.

Make ye sure to each his own

That he reap where he hath sown;

By the peace among Our peoples let men know we serve the Lord!

Hear now a song—a song of broken interludes—
A song of little cunning; of a singer nothing worth.
Through the naked words and mean
May ye see the truth between
As the singer knew and touched it in the ends of all the Earth!

THE COASTWISE LIGHTS

III

THE SWINGING, SMOKING SEAS

Our brows are bound with spindrift and the weed is on
our knees;
Our loins are battered 'neath us by the swinging, smoking
seas.

IV

ON THE LINELESS, LEVEL FLOORS

Through the endless summer evenings, on the lineless, level
floors.

V

THE COASTWISE LIGHTS OF ENGLAND

Come up, come in from Eastward, from the guardports of
the Morn!
Beat up, beat in from Southerly, O gipsies of the Horn!
Swift shuttles of an Empire's loom that weave us, main to
main,
The Coastwise Lights of England give you welcome back
again!

THE SWINGING, SMOKING SEAS

ON THE LINELESS,
LEVEL FLOORS

W. HEATH ROBINSON

THE COASTWISE LIGHTS
OF ENGLAND

W. HEATH ROBINSON

THE COASTWISE LIGHTS

Our brows are bound with spindrift and the weed
is on our knees;
Our loins are battered 'neath us by the swinging,
smoking seas.
From reef and rock and skerry—over headland,
ness, and voe—
The Coastwise Lights of England watch the ships
of England go!

Through the endless summer evenings, on the lineless, level floors;
Through the yelling Channel tempest when the siren hoots and roars—
By day the dipping house-flag and by night the rocket's trail—
As the sheep that graze behind us so we know them where they hail.

We bridge across the dark and bid the helmsman have a care,
The flash that wheeling inland wakes his sleeping wife to prayer;
From our vexed eyries, head to gale, we bind in burning chains
The lover from the sea-rim drawn—his love in English lanes.

We greet the clippers wing-and-wing that race the Southern wool;

We warn the crawling cargo-tanks of Bremen, Leith, and Hull;

To each and all our equal lamp at peril of the sea—

The white wall-sided warships or the whalers of Dundee!

Come up, come in from Eastward, from the guard-
ports of the Morn!
Beat up, beat in from Southerly, O gipsies of the
Horn!
Swift shuttles of an Empire's loom that weave us,
main to main,
The Coastwise Lights of England give you wel-
come back again!

Go, get you gone up-Channel with the sea-crust
on your plates;
Go, get you into London with the burden of your
freights!
Haste, for they talk of Empire there, and say, if
any seek,
The Lights of England sent you and by silence
shall ye speak!

THE SONG OF THE DEAD

THE SONG OF THE DEAD

VI

CAME THE WHISPER, CAME THE VISION

Came the Whisper, came the Vision, came the Power with
the Need,
Till the Soul that is not man's soul was lent us to lead.

VII

THEN THE LAST WATER DRIED

Then the wood failed—then the food failed—then the last
water dried—
In the faith of little children we lay down and died.

VIII

ON THE SAND-DRIFT—ON THE VELDT-SIDE

On the sand-drift—on the veldt-side—in the fern-scrub we
lay,
That our sons might follow after by the bones on the way.

IX

FOLLOW AFTER

Follow after—follow after—for the harvest is sown:
By the bones about the wayside ye shall come to your own!

CAME THE WHISPER,
CAME THE VISION

THEN THE LAST
WATER DRIED

HEATH
ROBINSON

ON THE SAND-DRIFT—ON THE VELDT-SIDE

FOLLOW AFTER

WHEN DRAKE WENT DOWN
TO THE HORN

W. HEATH ROBINSON

AND SHE CALLS US,
STILL UNFED

HEATH
ROBINSON

LORD GOD, WE HA' PAID
IN FULL

W. HEATH
ROBINSON

BUT DROPS OUR DEAD
ON THE SAND

W. HEATH. ROBINSON

X

WHEN DRAKE WENT DOWN TO THE HORN

When Drake went down to the Horn,
And England was crowned thereby.

XI

SHE CALLS US, STILL UNFED

We have fed our sea for a thousand years,
  And she calls us, still unfed,
Though there's never a wave of all her waves
  But marks our English dead.

XII

LORD GOD, WE HA' PAID IN FULL!

If blood be the price of admiralty,
  Lord God, we ha' paid in full!

XIII

BUT DROPS OUR DEAD ON THE SAND

There's never a flood goes shoreward now
  But lifts a keel we manned;
There's never an ebb goes seaward now
  But drops our dead on the sand—
But slinks our dead on the sands forlore,
  From the Ducies to the Swin.

Hear now the Song of the Dead—in the North
by the torn berg-edges—
They that look still to the Pole, asleep by their
hide-stripped sledges.
Song of the Dead in the South—in the sun by
their skeleton horses,
Where the warrigal whimpers and bays through
the dust of the sere river-courses.

Song of the Dead in the East—in the heat-rotted
jungle hollows,
Where the dog-ape barks in the kloof—in the
brake of the buffalo-wallows.
Song of the Dead in the West—in the Barrens,
the waste that betrayed them,
Where the wolverine tumbles their packs from the
camp and the grave-mound they made them;
Hear now the Song of the Dead!

We were dreamers, dreaming greatly, in the man-
stifled town;
We yearned beyond the sky-line where the strange
roads go down.
Came the Whisper, came the Vision, came the
Power with the Need,
Till the Soul that is not man's soul was lent us
to lead.
As the deer breaks—as the steer breaks—from
the herd where they graze,
In the faith of little children we went on our
ways.

Then the wood failed—then the food failed—then
the last water dried—
In the faith of little children we lay down and
died.
On the sand-drift—on the veldt-side—in the fern-
scrub we lay,
That our sons might follow after by the bones
on the way.
Follow after—follow after! We have watered the
root,
And the bud has come to blossom that ripens for
fruit!

Follow after—we are waiting, by the trails that
we lost,
For the sounds of many footsteps, for the tread
of a host.
Follow after—follow after—for the harvest is
sown:
By the bones about the wayside ye shall come to
your own!

When Drake went down to the Horn
And England was crowned thereby,
'Twixt seas unsailed and shores unhailed
Our Lodge—our Lodge was born
(*And England was crowned thereby!*)

Which never shall close again

By day nor yet by night,

While man shall take his life to stake

At risk of shoal or main

(*By day nor yet by night*)

But standeth even so
As now we witness here,
While men depart, of joyful heart,
Adventure for to know
(As now bear witness here!)

We have fed our sea for a thousand years
  And she calls us, still unfed,
Though there's never a wave of all her waves
  But marks our English dead:
We have strawed our best to the weed's unrest
  To the shark and the sheering gull.
If blood be the price of admiralty,
  Lord God, we ha' paid in full!

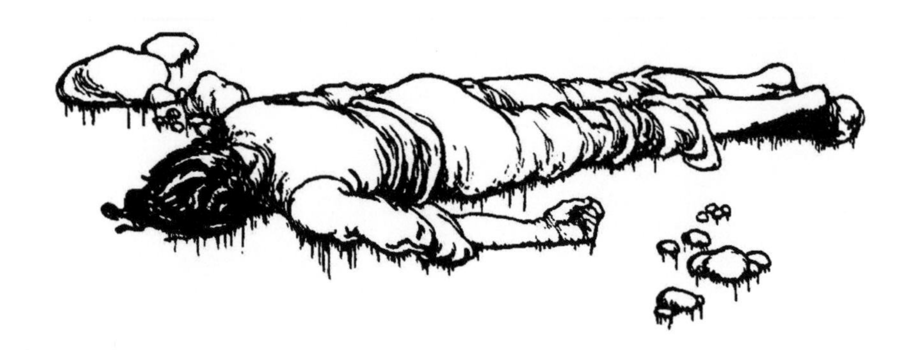

There's never a flood goes shoreward now
  But lifts a keel we manned;
There's never an ebb goes seaward now
  But drops our dead on the sand—
But slinks our dead on the sands forlore,
  From the Ducies to the Swin.
If blood be the price of admiralty,
If blood be the price of admiralty,
  Lord God, we ha' paid it in!

We must feed our sea for a thousand years,
  For that is our doom and pride,
As it was when they sailed with the *Golden Hind*,
  Or the wreck that struck last tide—
Or the wreck that lies on the spouting reef
  Where the ghastly blue-lights flare.
If blood be the price of admiralty,
If blood be the price of admiralty,
If blood be the price of admiralty,
  Lord God, we ha' bought it fair!

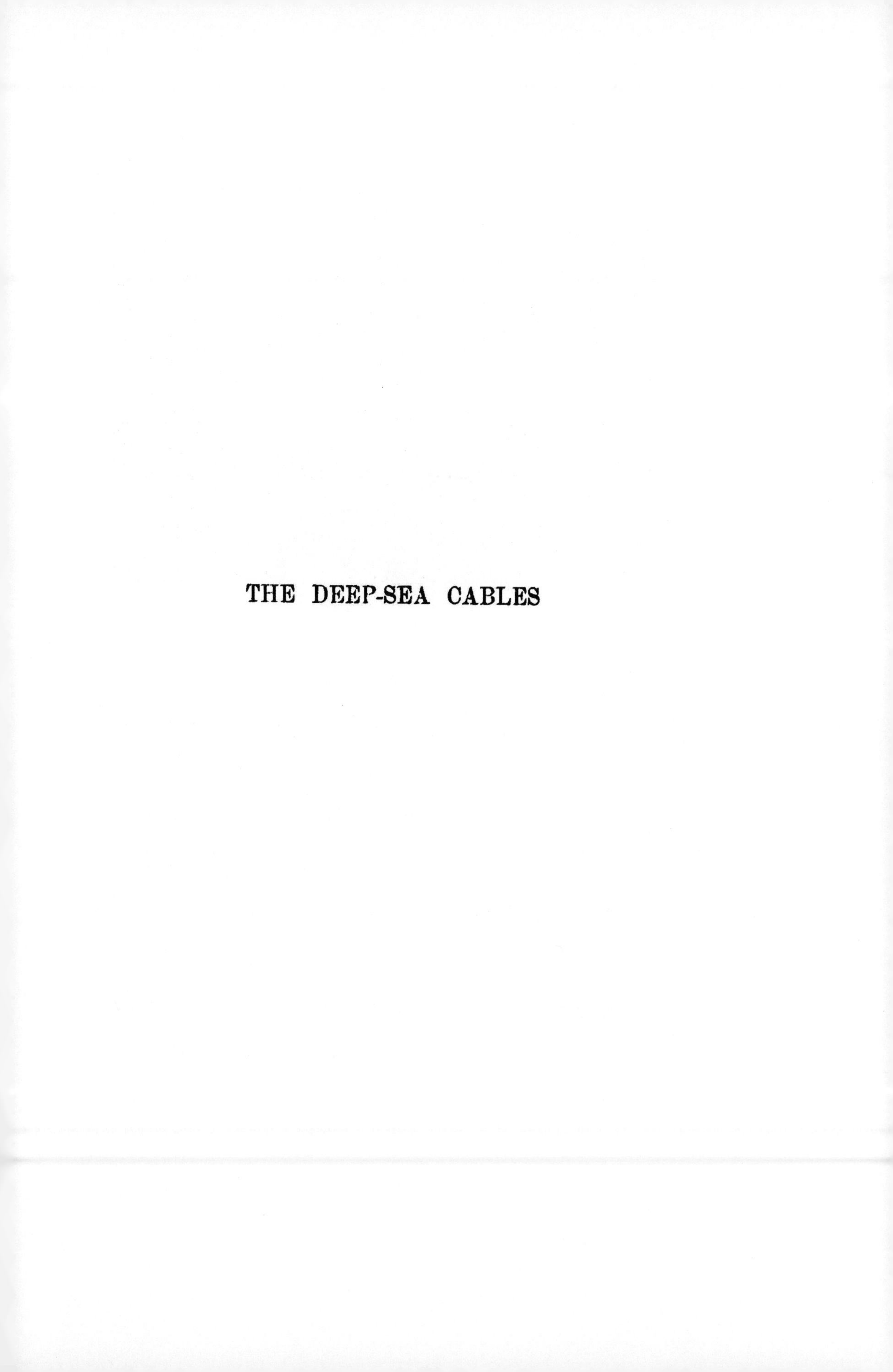

THE DEEP-SEA CABLES

XIV

THE WRECKS DISSOLVE ABOVE US

The wrecks dissolve above us; their dust drops down from
afar—
Down to the dark, to the utter dark, where the blind white
sea-snakes are.

XV

IN THE WOMB OF THE WORLD

Here in the womb of the world—here on the tie-ribs of
earth
Words, and the words of men, flicker and flutter and beat—
Warning, sorrow and gain, salutation and mirth—
For a Power troubles the Still that has neither voice nor
feet.

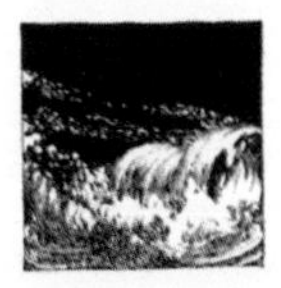

THE WRECKS DISSOLVE ABOVE US

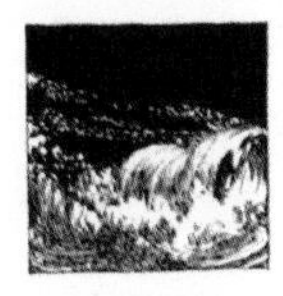

IN THE WOMB OF THE WORLD

THE DEEP-SEA CABLES

D 2

The wrecks dissolve above us; their dust drops
down from afar—
Down to the dark, to the utter dark, where the
blind white sea-snakes are.
There is no sound, no echo of sound, in the deserts
of the deep,
Or the great grey level plains of ooze where the
shell-burred cables creep.

Here in the womb of the world—here on the tie-
ribs of earth
Words, and the words of men, flicker and flutter
and beat—
Warning, sorrow and gain, salutation and
mirth—
For a Power troubles the Still that has neither
voice nor feet.

They have wakened the timeless Things; they have
killed their father Time;
Joining hands in the gloom, a league from the
last of the sun.
Hush! Men talk to-day o'er the waste of the
ultimate slime,
And a new Word runs between: whispering,
'Let us be one!'

XVI

WE THAT WERE BRED OVERSEAS

Those that have stayed at thy knees, Mother, go call
them in—
We that were bred overseas wait and would speak with
our kin.
Not in the dark do we fight—haggle and flout and gibe;
Selling our love for a price, loaning our hearts for a bribe.

WE THAT WERE BRED
OVERSEAS

THE SONG OF THE SONS

One from the ends of the earth—gifts at an open
door—
Treason has much, but we, Mother, thy sons have
more!
From the whine of a dying man, from the snarl
of a wolf-pack freed,
Turn, and the world is thine. Mother, be proud
of thy seed!
Count, are we feeble or few? Hear, is our speech
so rude?
Look, are we poor in the land? Judge, are we
men of The Blood?

Those that have stayed at thy knees, Mother, go
call them in—
We that were bred overseas wait and would speak
with our kin.
Not in the dark do we fight—haggle and flout
and gibe;
Selling our love for a price, loaning our hearts for
a bribe.
Gifts have we only to-day—Love without promise
or fee—
Hear, for thy children speak, from the uttermost
parts of the sea!

THE SONG OF THE CITIES

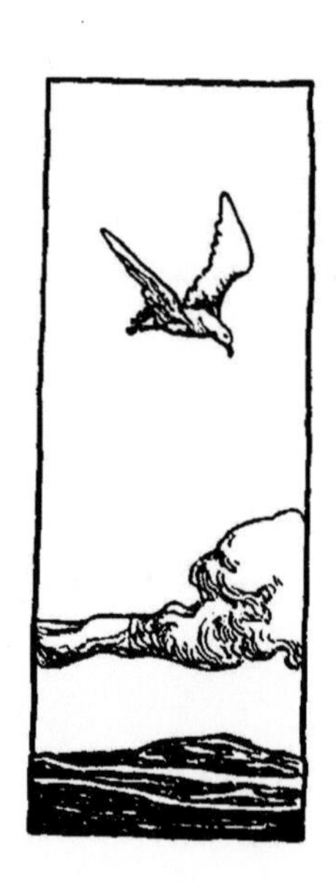

XVII. BOMBAY

XVIII. CALCUTTA

XIX. MADRAS

XX. RANGOON

XXI. SINGAPORE

XXII. HONG-KONG

XXIII. HALIFAX

XXIV. QUEBEC AND MONTREAL

XXV. CAPETOWN

XXVI. MELBOURNE

XXVII. SYDNEY

XXVIII. HOBART

XXIX. AUCKLAND

BOMBAY

CALCUTTA

W
HEATH
ROBINSON

MADRAS

RANGOON

SINGAPORE

HONG-KONG

HALIFAX

QUEBEC AND
MONTREAL

CAPETOWN

MELBOURNE

W HEATH ROBINSON

SYDNEY

HOBART

AUCKLAND

THE SONG OF THE CITIES

BOMBAY

Royal and Dower-royal, I the Queen
  Fronting thy richest sea with richer hands—
A thousand mills roar through me where I glean
  All races from all lands.

CALCUTTA

Me the Sea-captain loved, the River built,

Wealth sought and Kings adventured life to hold.

Hail, England! I am Asia—Power on silt,

Death in my hands, but Gold!

MADRAS

Clive kissed me on the mouth and eyes and brow,
  Wonderful kisses, so that I became
Crowned above Queens—a withered beldame now,
  Brooding on ancient fame.

RANGOON

Hail, Mother! Do they call me rich in trade?
Little care I, but hear the shorn priest drone,
And watch my silk-clad lovers, man by maid,
Laugh 'neath my Shwe Dagon.

SINGAPORE

Hail, Mother! East and West must seek my aid
  Ere the spent gear may dare the ports afar.
The second doorway of the wide world's trade
  Is mine to loose or bar.

HONG-KONG

Hail, Mother! Hold me fast; my Praya sleeps
Under innumerable keels to-day.
Yet guard (and landward), or to-morrow sweeps
Thy warships down the bay!

HALIFAX

Into the mist my guardian prows put forth,
  Behind the mist my virgin ramparts lie,
The Warden of the Honour of the North,
  Sleepless and veiled am I!

Peace is our portion. Yet a whisper rose,
  Foolish and causeless, half in jest, half hate.
Now wake we and remember mighty blows,
  And, fearing no man, wait!

From East to West the circling word has passed,
  Till West is East beside our land-locked blue;
From East to West the tested chain holds fast,
  The well-forged link rings true!

CAPETOWN

Hail! Snatched and bartered oft from hand to
hand,
I dream my dream, by rock and heath and pine,
Of Empire to the northward. Ay, one land
From Lion's Head to Line!

MELBOURNE

Greeting! Nor fear nor favour won us place,
  Got between greed of gold and dread of drouth,
Loud-voiced and reckless as the wild tide-race
  That whips our harbour-mouth!

SYDNEY

Greeting! My birth-stain have I turned to good;
  Forcing strong wills perverse to steadfastness;
The first flush of the tropics in my blood,
  And at my feet Success!

BRISBANE

The northern stirp beneath the southern skies—

I build a Nation for an Empire's need,

Suffer a little, and my land shall rise,

Queen over lands indeed!

HOBART

Man's love first found me; man's hate made me
Hell;
For my babes' sake I cleansed those infamies.
Earnest for leave to live and labour well,
God flung me peace and ease.

AUCKLAND

Last, loneliest, loveliest, exquisite, apart—

On us, on us the unswerving season smiles,

Who wonder 'mid our fern why men depart

To seek the Happy Isles!

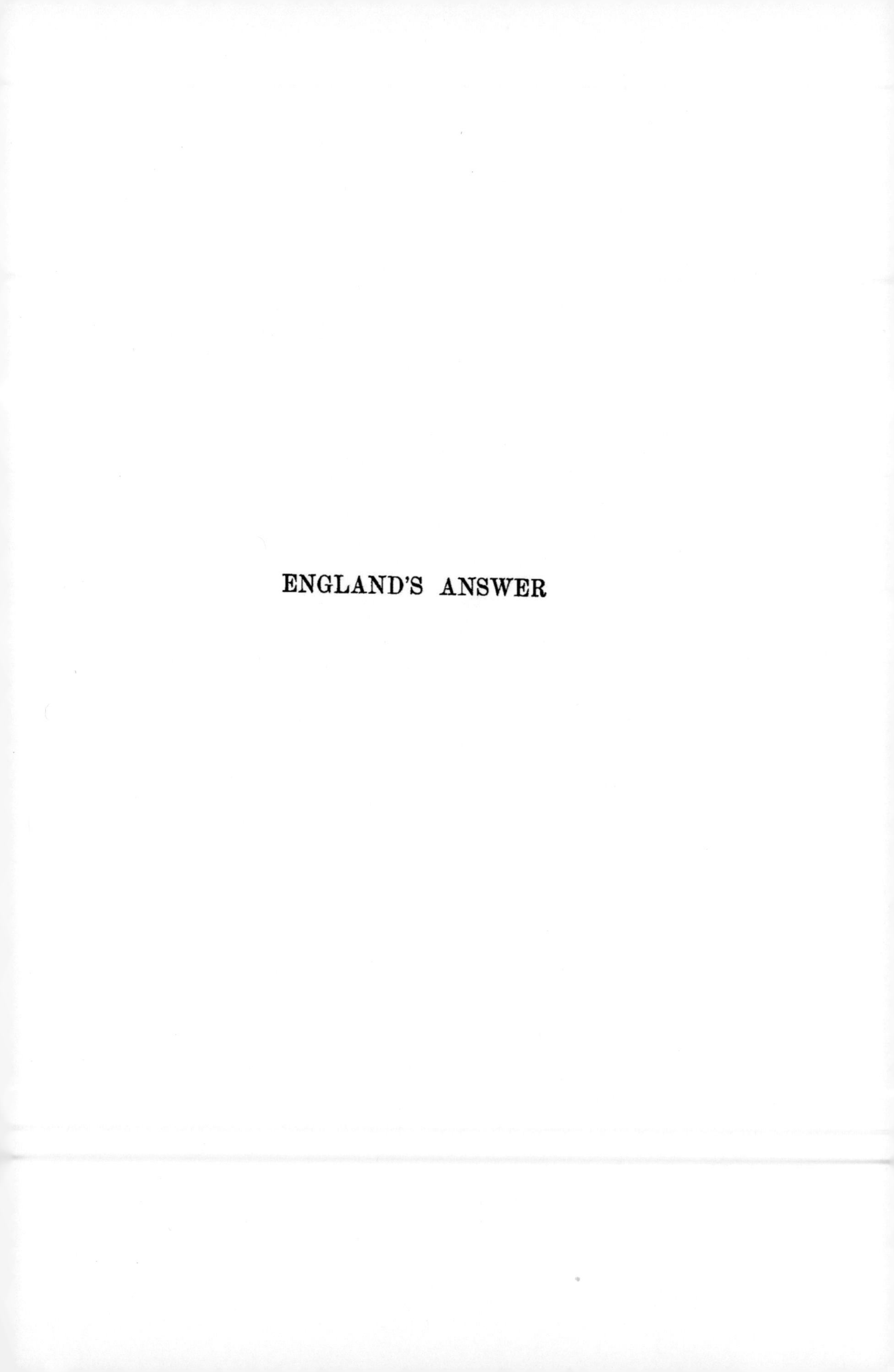

ENGLAND'S ANSWER

XXX

MY ARM IS NOTHING WEAK, MY STRENGTH IS NOT GONE BY

Deeper than speech our love, stronger than life our tether,
But we do not fall on the neck nor kiss when we come together.
My arm is nothing weak, my strength is not gone by;
Sons, I have borne many sons, but my dugs are not dry.

MY ARM IS NOTHING WEAK.
MY STRENGTH IS NOT
GONE BY

ENGLAND'S ANSWER

Truly ye come of The Blood; slower to bless than
to ban;
Little used to lie down at the bidding of any
man.
Flesh of the flesh that I bred, bone of the bone
that I bare;

Stark as your sons shall be—stern as your fathers
were.
Deeper than speech our love, stronger than life our
tether,
But we do not fall on the neck nor kiss when we
come together.

My arm is nothing weak, my strength is not gone by;

Sons, I have borne many sons, but my dugs are not dry.

Look, I have made ye a place and opened wide the doors,

That ye may talk together, your Barons and Councillors—
Wards of the Outer March, Lords of the Lower Seas,
Ay, talk to your grey mother that bore you on her knees!—

That ye may talk together, brother to brother's
face—
Thus for the good of your peoples—thus for the
Pride of the Race.
Also, we will make promise. So long as The Blood
endures,

I shall know that your good is mine: ye shall feel
that my strength is yours:
In the day of Armageddon, at the last great fight
of all,
That Our House stand together and the pillars do
not fall.

Draw now the threefold knot firm on the ninefold
bands,
And the Law that ye make shall be law after the
rule of your lands.
This for the waxen Heath, and that for the Wattle-
bloom,

This for the Maple-leaf, and that for the southern
Broom.
The Law that ye make shall be law and I do not
press my will,
Because ye are Sons of The Blood and call me
Mother still.

Now must ye speak to your kinsmen and they
must speak to you,
After the use of the English, in straight-flung
words and few.
Go to your work and be strong, halting not in
your ways,

Baulking the end half-won for an instant dole of praise.

Stand to your work and be wise—certain of sword and pen,

Who are neither children nor Gods, but men in a world of men!

Printed in Great Britain
by Amazon